PROMOTIONS ARE NOT SERVED AT THE DELI COUNTER

MICHAEL PATTERSON

Promotions Are Not Served at the Deli Counter

DEDICATION

To my dad, who taught me the importance of hard work, dependability, and making your own opportunities for success. He would not have understood why I would need to write a book to tell other people how to do the same. But I do believe he would have enjoyed reading it.

ACKNOWLEDGEMENTS

Thank you to everyone for your assistance and support throughout the entire process of creating this book.

Special thanks to my wife Ann for her support during this process and for her last minute edits and corrections. I know our schedules give us little time together, and the last thing you want is for me to be putting together a book.

Thank you to Brian H. for reviewing a rough draft of this book and offering your insight, and to Marge for your meticulous review. Thanks to everyone I work with: JoAnn, Debbie, Aimee, Michele, Christine, and Randi for putting up with me talking about writing "the book" month after month, and also for enduring the endless amount of my analogies and sayings; many of which have wound up in here.

Last but not least, thank you to Kathy Pitts and Lorie Sfugarus for taking a chance on me and starting my training career.

CONTENTS

Promotions Are Not Served at the Deli Counter

INTRODUCTION

I was buttoning up my white dress shirt and tying my blue tie on the morning of August 24, 1989; preparing for my second interview for an entry-level teller position at Horizon Financial. This day will be remembered for two important moments in history:

1. Baseball Commissioner Bart Giamatti suspended Pete Rose for life for gambling on major league baseball games, and

2. I started my path towards a 20+ year career in banking.

Just as I'm sure Pete Rose didn't fully realize the ramifications that day would have twenty years later, neither did I. Seventeen years old and only two months removed from the safety zone called high school, I had no idea what the business world had in store for me.

Over the years I have worked my way up from being a teller making a robust $5.35 an hour (a quarter an hour raise would come three months later) to heading the training department of a $1.3 billion, 300 employee credit union. I've had my share of successes and failures; been turned down for promotions I thought were in the bag, and received offers when I wasn't even actively looking for them. Along the way I have learned lessons which I have shared with participants in my training classes, and now feel the need to share with you.

I have read many books on business over the years from people respected in the field such as Dale Carnegie, Zig Zigler, Steven Covey, and John Maxwell. The bookstore shelves are stocked with books geared towards aspiring leaders who are poised for greatness. But where are the books for those just entering the workforce, aspiring to get a paycheck and survive to get another one two weeks later? I wanted to write a book which I would have liked to have read when I was graduating high school and entering the business world over twenty years ago.

This book is about ways in which you can better position yourself to achieve your goals at work. We will look at the common mistakes employees make, and examine the pitfalls into which they tend to get trapped and find the proverbial ladder needed to climb out.

This book will be part funny, sad, ironic, and sometimes sarcastic. While understanding the process of succeeding in the workforce, it will use analogies from politics, sports, entertainment and more. It will inform and provoke. It will provide the education for employees in the corporate world you didn't receive in high school or college.

I hope you find it useful.

Promotions Are Not Served at the Deli Counter

1

IF YOU WANT THE FAIR WAY, LOOK FOR THE GOLF COURSE

"Expecting the world to be fair to you because you are a good person is like expecting the bull not to charge because you are a vegetarian." – Author Unknown

Oftentimes in work, one person's decision makes a difference. Just one person can make, or break, an individual's career in their organization. How is it that one person can hold so much power over another one's career? Is it fair? Is it right? Could it be a conflict of interest?

Consider the story of Katherine Harris and the 2000 presidential election. As Secretary of State for the State of Florida, Harris had what is usually considered the ceremonial responsibility of certifying her state's elections. However, the 2000 presidential election between then Texas Governor George Bush and then Vice-President Al Gore was unlike any election seen before.

The implementation of confusing butterfly punch-card ballots in the southern counties of Florida created a controversy. Allegedly, voters were so confused reading the ballot that thousands of votes intended for Al Gore were actually casted for third-party candidate Pat Buchanan. Additionally, some elderly voters had difficulty punching the little perforated box on the card all of the way through. The actual result of the election was in such contradiction of scientific exit polls, most of the networks called the state for Al Gore, before retracting and changing the call for George Bush. It was such a mess; Al Gore actually called George Bush the night of the election to concede defeat, only to rescind the concession about an hour later.

This brings us up to Katherine Harris, who had been named the co-chairperson of Gov. Bush's Florida campaign the year before the election. Harris certified Bush received more votes in the election than Gore, thus winning all of Florida's electoral votes; enough to win the presidency. Under enormous pressure, she softened her stance and allowed counties in south Florida to conduct hand recounts of each ballot. However, Secretary Harris implemented a deadline which would make the completion of the recounts virtually impossible.

In the end, Bush officially won Florida by a mere 537 votes, therefore, winning Florida's electoral votes — and the Presidency of the United States. [1]

The debate regarding how fair the presidency was decided still continues years later. Individuals' stance on the issue will decide more on their political affiliations than the actual details of the situation. This is also how issues of fairness play themselves out in corporations throughout the country. Your concept of what is "fair" is usually determined by whether you (or the person you support) got the promotion, the raise, permission to leave early, or whatever else he or she was seeking. If you got what you wanted, the decision was fair; if not, it was not.

Unfortunately, people go through work acting like a racehorse in the Kentucky Derby. Those horses are equipped with blinders, a synthetic hood equipped with cups which are attached to encircle the horses' eyes. This makes it virtually impossible to see anything behind or beside the horse. Trainers believe wearing this will make the horse focus solely on the finish line, avoiding the distraction of the crowd or other horses. Employees who wear blinders are also oblivious to anyone or anything around them. They are only focused on their goal or finish line. Because of this, when an employee is not afforded the promotion, increase, or other perk they cherish, he or she cannot see the other factors which went into the ultimate decision. They only see the decision as being unjust, "not fair."

This recently happened at my job when one woman (Kelly) was upset that another woman (Paula) was promoted ahead of her. Kelly's complaint centered on the fact she was with the organization for 15 months, which was six months more than Paula. What Kelly didn't know was while this was her first job at a financial institution, Paula had almost three years of experience at another bank. She has already held the position they were both applying for, and only left that bank because her husband had to be relocated for his job. When you put all the facts together, the situation doesn't seem as unfair for Kelly as it may have originally appeared.

Let's go back and revisit how "fair" the result of the 2000 election was for Al Gore. From 1789 to 2008, there have been 56 elections held for President of the United States. In only three of those elections a man won the presidency while losing his home state. James Polk became the first man to do this way back in 1844, Woodrow Wilson in 1916, and Richard Nixon in 1968.[2] (Actually this is a technicality. President Nixon lost New York, a state he moved to only four years prior to the election. However he did win California which was the state he spent most of his life.)

Prior to being elected Vice President, Al Gore served eight years as a senator from the state of Tennessee. Before that, Mr. Gore served six years in Congress representing Tennessee's 4th congressional district. In the 2000 presidential election, Al Gore lost the state of Tennessee by just over 80,000 votes. By winning the state, George Bush was awarded all 11 of its electoral votes. While partisans point to the controversy which ensued in Florida as the reason for Al Gore's loss, he could have avoided the mess entirely by simply winning his home state.

Employees in every office, in every state, complain every day, about their perceived lack of fairness. The truth of the matter is employees rarely have complete control over their own destiny. Anytime another individual has control over your occupational fate, questions can arise regarding which influences helped lead to his/her decisions. As an employee, you must honestly make an effort to do everything in your power to make that decision end up in your favor. It is far easier to do average work and complain about not getting a promotion than it is to give maximum effort, produce results, and give your manager no choice but to choose you for the job.

In their book *Becoming the Obvious Choice*, authors Bryan Dodge and David Cottrell provide readers with sound advice on how to prepare for job advancement opportunities.[3] If you do what you need to do, than your supervisor will have nobody else to look at for the promotion than you. In essence, you have become the obvious choice for the position. I've come across dozens of employees looking for promotions over the years. All of them were able to provide me with reasons why they thought they should get the promotion. A lot of them sounded convincing. After they were done telling me what they thought of their qualifications, I would ask them this question: "What would your current boss tell me if I asked him or her why you should be promoted?" This is usually where you can tell the serious contenders from the pretenders. The serious candidates would always be able to tell me how their supervisor thinks they are promotable, and tell me with the same vigor and conviction which they told me only moments before. The pretenders would stammer and stall. They may make up an excuse how their manager doesn't really like them, or the job is going to go to someone else, even though that person wasn't nearly as qualified as they were. I'd probably even get the classic line how it just wasn't fair.

Even if you do everything you need to do in order to succeed, sometimes things happen which are beyond your control. As the saying goes "timing is everything", and maybe your time and the company's doesn't mesh up. I talked with a female employee who finally had a promotional opportunity become available at her branch. She was qualified for the position, and would have been a great choice for her supervisor. This employee was six months pregnant at the time, and didn't think it was the right time to switch jobs and take on more responsibilities. Unfortunately for her, the timing just wasn't right.

During the recent economic recession, many companies capped their annual increases at small percentages – if they even offered them at all. I knew former colleagues of mine who put in maximum effort, exceeded goals, and received complimentary performance reviews only to be rewarded with a 1.5% raise. Ouch. I know they didn't think the raise amount was fair, but there was nothing to be done about it. But some people should be so lucky. In June 2009, Philadelphia City Council mandated city workers making $35,000 or more take one unpaid day off a month in order to cut costs as the city was facing serious budget woes. That unpaid day off equated to a 4.6% pay cut for the average worker. Again, it may not be fair, but those were the harsh realities of working during a recession.

One of my favorite sayings in work is "it is what it is" I love saying "it is what it is". Some people think it's an illogical phrase which doesn't really mean anything. I think it says it all. To me "it is what it is" tells people they don't have to overanalyze the situation, don't have to look for a hidden meaning, there is no great conspiracy theory. Some things need no explanation; they are really the way they seem. I think the phrase can be traced back to Ockham 's razor which is a philosophy meaning the simplest answer is usually the correct one. No fuss, no muss. One wise philosopher looks at the glass as half full. Another wise philosopher looks at it as half empty. My grandfather looked at the glass and wondered where he left his teeth.

The truth of the matter is, work is a lot like life overall. Sometimes it just plain sucks. There are perfect employees who do the right things and never get the recognition they deserve. Then there are people who take shortcuts, become lazy when the boss isn't looking, and get promoted up through the corporation. What is comforting to know is those situations are the exception, not the norm. It is comforting to know that, unless of course *you* happen to be the perfect employee who gets passed over. I used to worry about a lot of things when I was younger until I realized I spent too much time worrying. Why waste time worrying over the things you can't control? That time would be better suited making strides to affect the things you can control. Sometimes things that happen at work really aren't fair. Move on. Spend time making yourself a better employee and the breaks will come your way. Over the following chapters we will look at ways you can do just that.

2

THERE ARE NO PARTICIPATION TROPHIES IN THE WORKPLACE

Like most male, American school kids, I played little league baseball as a child. Just like Girl Scout cookies and McDonald's Shamrock Shakes, moms and dads registering their sons for little league was the sign to show spring was right around the corner.

A few weeks after registration, your coach would call you saying you were on his team. Then practice begins, and pretty soon you are getting your uniform, decorated with an advertisement of the local pizza parlor or sandwich shop. Before you know it, there's picture day, opening day, and a couple months of games. You win some, and lose some (we usually won some and lost a lot). When the team played a good game, the coach usually bought everyone water ice - even if you lost! At the end of the season, the best teams made the playoffs. The players of the teams in the finals got trophies, with the champions' trophies dwarfing those of the runners-up.

This is the understanding I grew up with. To me, my friends, and our parents, this was the acceptable norm. Nobody would expect anything different. Trophies went to the champions. Individuals were acknowledged and rewarded for winning. Since most winning seasons were the result of dedication and hard work, a correlation could be made that individuals were rewarded for dedication and hard work. Of course, more than one team could have hardworking dedicated individuals on it. So you also learned the value of teamwork. Multiple teams can be made up of hardworking, dedicated, individuals who work as a team. That's when you learn sometimes you need a little bit of luck, and opportunity, to be a winner.

Back in the early 1990s the philosophy I learned in little
league still held up. During this time I coached a wrestling
team consisting of 13-15 year olds. They were taught hard
work and dedication would produce results. Add in a little
bit of luck, and the ability to take advantage of your
opportunities, and those results would lead to wins and
championships. The top guys at the end of the season
competed for our team's most glamorous prize: the
"Outstanding Wrestler" award. In most years, competition
for the "OW" was fierce. It was not uncommon to see more
than one young wrestler on the team with an undefeated
record and a ton of pins. But the understanding was
always only one wrestler would snag the big trophy at the
end of the year. Just like the workplace, where multiple
highly qualified applicants with impressive resumes fought
for the same position, somebody was going home
disappointed. All of this changed, however, with the
growing popularity of the politically correct "participation
trophy."

Sports leagues throughout the country routinely hand out
"participation trophies" during their year-end awards
banquets. Some attempt to make these pieces of gold
painted aluminum and plastic appear to have more

prestige by calling them "achievement trophies." I guess in the extremely complicated life of an elementary school kid, coming out to practice most days and putting on a uniform for game days without quitting is an achievement. Some organizations further inflate their importance by making participation trophies as big, or even (gasp) bigger than those awarded to players for achievement. Oops, I mean, *real* achievement.

In his bestselling book, *Muzzled*, Michael Smerconish writes about participation trophies and how they relate to the political correctness of America.[4] While Mr. Smerconish makes a great point, my issue isn't one of political correctness. My concern is the message it is sending children who grow up to be adults who join the workplace. The message I grew up with of dedication, hard work, teamwork, opportunity, and a little luck has been replaced. The new message is don't worry, just show up, "participate", and be rewarded.

While it may still be popular in youth sports leagues, participation trophies don't get handed out in the workplace. In business, the same values I learned in little league still create the ingredient for success: dedication, hard work, opportunity, teamwork, and a little luck. Let's take a look at each of the five ingredients more closely.

Dedication

There is an old joke about how much dedication is required to make a breakfast of eggs and bacon. "The chicken had to put in some hard work", the joke goes; "but the pig had to really be dedicated!"

How dedicated are you at work? How much are you willing to give? Let's say you work in an office where someone needs to stay late on a regular basis. It was your turn the day before, and you stayed. Today is Sally's turn, but she had to leave work early because her child was sent home sick from school. Your boss asks you to stay again today. You have no real plans yourself right after work. Do you agree to stay or argue you stayed last night? Do you name another co-worker who should stay? Do you try and broker a deal with your boss? Sometimes, employees expect more dedication from their employer than they are willing to give themselves.

What defines dedication? As an employee, you don't need to work longer and harder hours to prove you're dedicated.

In all honesty, you don't have to be dedicated to the institution you work for or the job you currently hold. All you need to do is be dedicated to yourself, and to producing your best effort.

Preparing yourself to be dedicated to providing your best effort requires you to take a quick self-assessment. This can be accomplished by asking two questions:

Am I providing my best effort each and every day?
What can I do which can increase my effort?

Determine your effort by starting at… well, the start. A bad start to the day will almost always impede your success for the entire day. Over the course of 44 Super Bowl games played, no team has ever come back to win after trailing by more than 10 points. In the biggest single game in all of sports, no team has ever succeeded when faced with a bad start. You can overcome your own bad starts by recognizing and correcting the issues which cause the bad start in the first place.

To be dedicated to providing your best effort, start with the basics. Get a good night sleep. If you feel sluggish and unproductive while only getting five hours of sleep each night, try to get six or seven. Leave your house five minutes earlier in the morning to avoid the hassle of trying to hurry to avoid being late. I once had a female in her early twenties work for me. She was habitually late to work. That wasn't too good for her, as my biggest pet peeve at work is lateness. When a person is constantly late to anything, especially work, they are telling me two things; their time is more important than my time, and they are too lazy to get their act together and get where they need to be at the time they need to be there. So after a pattern of lateness over a few weeks, I sat down with my employee to stress the importance of her reporting to work on time. I asked simply if she knew what time she needed to be in work. To her credit, she knew 8:30 was her scheduled time to report, and it took her twenty minutes from her house to the office. Now on average, this girl was close to twenty minutes late, which meant she wasn't leaving her house until it was time for her to have already been in the office. I told her simply she needed to leave her house earlier. When she told me how much she needed to do in the morning to get ready for work I told her she obviously needed to wake up earlier. If that was an issue, I told her, she could consider getting to bed earlier the night before.

Now it's not my responsibility to put a curfew on my employees, and I could see she had gotten annoyed. The simple fact is I didn't care when she went to sleep or woke up. All I cared about was her being on time each morning. The lateness's were completely under her control. If she was dedicated to getting to work on time, she would have found a way to do it.

Dedicate yourself to learn something new each day. Make it a point to watch or read something educational each day. When reading a book or magazine, read with the intent to teach. During leadership training, I conduct an exercise asking participants to list the last three books they read. The participants need to tell me one skill, idea, or concept learned from the book which they can apply to their job. You can learn an applicable function from almost any book read.

I had an employee once tell me he didn't know enough about mortgages. He attended my training class, but still had questions. The questions he had were more about government regulations and practices than our bank's specific policies and procedures. I told him to search for information online and read the real estate section of the

Sunday newspaper. These were ways in which he could have taken the initiative to learn something new, even if it is outside of his normal work hours. Depending upon your line of work, I am sure there are things you can do outside of work to dedicate yourself to improve.

Hard Work

Nobody ever said work was supposed to be easy and fun. This is the predominate reason why individuals are paid to work, and pay others to "play." What is the first difference between going to work and going to Disney World? You get paid to go to work, and you pay to go to Disney. In fact, most people pay more for a one-week vacation than they would have earned in that week working. A one-week vacation to a four-star Caribbean resort; including hotel, air from Philadelphia, plus food, will cost about $1700 per person in 2010. Unless you have a job earning almost $90,000 a year, you will have paid more money for your week away than you would have earned working!

In the workplace, employees advance because they possess a skill, trait, or knowledge, over other individuals. People hone those abilities through studying, retention, and practice. Many employees develop shortcuts which make their workload easier or quicker to accomplish. Oftentimes these shortcuts eliminate what the individual believes to be laborious tasks. However these steps insure the work was done as intended, eliminating mistakes and problems at the end.

During training, employees often like to tell of a shortcut they learned. When considering a shortcut, I always ask if it can accomplish two goals compared to the "long way." Can the task be completed with the same accuracy? Can the task be completed with the same cost (money and time)? Be aware all costs must be considered, including any backend costs. In banking, if a shortcut leaves someone more susceptible to fraud and loss, the backend costs could be enormous.

It really all does start with hard work. Very few things in your life will come easy. If you are one of those people who tend to have gifts fall in your lap, consider yourself extremely lucky – and extremely rare. Most people don't just wake up in the morning, roll out of bed, walk out the door, and become a success. One of the founders of our country, Thomas Jefferson once said "I am a great believer of luck, and find the harder I work the more I have of it."[5]

Mr. Jefferson knew a thing or two about hard work, as he worked at a feverish pace over just seventeen days to create the most important document in our country's history.

When I was coaching I had a saying which I would often throw out to my wrestlers; "Most people want to be a champion, but few want to prepare to be a champion." Being handed a large shiny trophy is fun. Practice is not. Spending time in the gym or running alongside the road isn't fun either. But the truth is, it is the effort and hard work you put in the gym and in practice which allows you to be in a position to get handed a large shiny trophy. At work, promotions and raises are the large shiny trophy.

According to Marketdata, a market research firm that has tracked diet products and programs since 1989, Americans spent $55 billion in 2007 on weight loss products. That figure is estimated to surpass $60 billion in 2010.[6] However, the top trainers and nutritionists in the country claim diet pills don't work. In fact, many have been found to be harmful to people who use them. They recommend a combination of proper diet and exercise to lose weight and maintain it. But that's hard work, and most people aren't interested in putting in the hard work, they only want to see the results. The truth is nothing comes easy.

Hard work is the key to many success stories. Often, the employee who worries about the details, produces high quality, and takes the time to get it right even if it means putting in the extra hours, is the one receiving the accolades from management. We'll talk more about hard work in the chapter "Everything I Needed to Know I Learned From Batman".

Teamwork

It would probably be safe to say the concept of teamwork has been around as long as man himself. You can imagine a prehistoric caveman knowing he could spear a bison to death all by himself, but then learning he needs the help of others to carry it back to cook and eat. Over 100,000 years later, developing the need for people to work together remains a priority for organizations throughout the country. Walk into your favorite bookstore and you will be sure to find dozens of books related to teamwork and teambuilding activities.

One of our founding fathers, Benjamin Franklin, once famously said "we must indeed all hang together, or must assuredly, we shall all hang separately."[7] In the workplace people have different roles and responsibilities. They also have various strengths and weaknesses. To be successful, teams parley each other's strengths to reduce their own weaknesses. This is the reason why teamwork is so important. Brett Favre holds the NFL record for most yards passing and touchdowns thrown.[8] He wouldn't have those records if not for the receivers who caught the passes, and the lineman whose job is was to block the pass rushers.

So if this sounds like an easy concept to grasp, why is there such an overabundance of books and resources to improve teambuilding skills at work? It is because in many workplaces people get rewarded for their individual accomplishments rather than those of the team. Your role at work can change from one year to the next. Your position is attained from years of developing skills, oftentimes at the expense of somebody else's aspirations. Everybody can aspire to become manager, or even CEO. In order to move up, employees must look for ways to showcase their talent and promote their successes. However success cannot be obtained without the help of others, and the person you help today may be the person helping you tomorrow.

Assume you work in an office where sales goals are extremely important. Joe is your top salesperson. Nobody is better at talking to new customers, referring products, and obtaining the sale than Joe. Praise is heaped on Joe; he receives quarterly awards and extra incentive pay. Your department reaches and shatters its annual sales goal, and is named "Department of the Year". All because of Joe. Well, maybe not *all* because of him. While it's true Joe was responsible for most of the new sales, he could not have done it without the help of his teammates – his co-workers. In addition to selling to new customers, employees are also responsible for servicing their existing customers. While this is part of Joe's job responsibilities, it is not his strongest suit. Instead, Joe's co-workers pick up his slack, allowing him to spend more time selling. What would happen if his co-workers were terrible at servicing customers? These customers would become dissatisfied, forcing employees to spend valuable time retaining existing customers as opposed to attracting new ones. Praise also must go to the people responsible for creating and marketing the products being sold. They provide Joe the necessary ammunition he needs to sell to new customers.

While Joe is the employee receiving most of the credit, he needs the support of his co-workers to get the job done; regardless of whether he realizes it or not! If a baseball player hits a three-run homerun in the bottom of the ninth to win the game by a run, he's the one getting the credit. He gets the postgame interview and gets his swing on ESPN *Sports Center*. But what about the two other players who found a way to get on base before he came up? If not for them, the star player's homerun wouldn't be the game winner. He might not even have gotten an at-bat. What about the fielder who made a big play the inning before to keep it to a two-run game in the first place? Everyone needs an assist from someone else to be successful.

Opportunity

There is an old saying instructing you whenever you hear opportunity knocking to be ready to answer the door. This is true because opportunity doesn't come around knocking too often. Opportunity is out there for everyone. Unfortunately, many people don't recognize it when it presents itself. There is an old story I like to tell classes about missed opportunity. As a disclaimer, I let people know it has a religious connotation to it; it is not meant to offend.

A very religious man was sitting in his house when a newscaster came on the radio warning of a hard rain which will create a great flood. Residents should evacuate. The man wasn't going anywhere, he was deeply religious and believed God would save him. The rains came down and two feet of water filled the streets. A man in a boat came by the house to rescue the man. The man wasn't going anywhere; "I am a religious man" he said "and God will save me." The floods reached unbelievable levels, and the man climbed outside to sit on his roof. Just then a helicopter flew by offering a rope to rescue the man. The man wouldn't grab on; "I am a religious man" he said "and God will save me." Eventually the floods encompassed the house and the man drowned. Upon reaching heaven, he was very upset and demanded a meeting with God. "I was deeply religious, and trusted you'd save me. You did nothing" he protested. "What do you mean nothing" God replied, "I sent you a radio newscast, a boat, and a helicopter."

As the story illustrates, opportunities may be provided in ways you are not expecting. While an opportunity may be a promotion, it may only be a new challenge or increased responsibility. It may allow you to gain experience, or prove to others your various skills and abilities. Opportunities do not guarantee an immediate increase in pay, and may require more work in the short term. Too many times employees pass up an opportunity because it requires more work for the same pay. What they don't realize is their manager is giving them an opportunity to learn a new skill or demonstrate the ability to perform a task, either of which would make them more promotable in the future.

Many employees miss the knock of opportunity because they believe in a bad mathematical equation:

$$O = \$$$

Opportunity = More Money

All opportunities do not come with financial rewards attached. As previously stated, opportunities in the workplace may require you to do more, take on extra responsibilities, increase work hours, or travel for no additional compensation. The opportunity is not financial, it is the ability to learn, develop, and demonstrate new skills which may be required for the future promotion. Employees may pass up these opportunities because they do not realize the instant gratification of a fatter check. Instead, they consider the extra workload as a detriment instead of an opportunity.

While everyone wants to make as much money as possible immediately, taking on these added responsibilities is an investment in your corporate future. As someone possibly new to the corporate world, you should concentrate on building your resume for future job advancement. Most employers want individuals with experience for higher level positions. By assigning added responsibilities, supervisors are providing their employees with a way to obtain this experience while still maintaining their current position. Consider it on-the-job training for your future job. While excelling in new responsibilities such as preparing a report or creating a work schedule reap no monetary rewards in the present, you are gaining valuable experience which makes you more promotable in the future. When interviewing for a future job which lists "ability to create a work schedule" as a job requirement, you can confirm you not only have the *ability*, you also have the *experience*. You took the opportunity to proactively become more promotable instead of waiting for the promotion to come to you. Keep this in mind when you read the next chapter.

In banking, tellers are the people who take customers' deposits and loan payments, make withdrawals, cash checks, etc. The head teller (or teller supervisor) has the added responsibilities of balancing the ATM machine and large cash vault. Many times the head teller will train a teller to be her "backup", capable of settling the ATM or vault in her absence. There is no added monetary compensation for this, only the added knowledge and experience of performing those duties. Because of this, sometimes employees balk at assuming the added responsibility; feeling used for doing someone else's job and not getting paid. This just isn't the case at all. Managers are using this as a "test run" to determine if the teller can perform the duties before being promoted. Consider this; if you are interviewing for a job, would it sound better to say you "*could* balance the vault" or you "*have* successfully balanced the vault many times"?

My advice is to take advantage of every opportunity you are given in an organization. On the job activities, training classes, books, and the internet are all excellent ways to learn and grow. Demonstrating the initiative to learn new things will make you promotable, either at not at your current job or another company. Also, take the time to make your own opportunities. Instead of waiting for opportunity to come knocking on your door, you could always drive over to opportunity's house instead. Once you have conquered your normal work duties, ask your supervisor for additional responsibilities. Managers love employees who show initiative. This is your opportunity to prove how dedicated you are to succeed by putting in additional hard work which may also help lessen the burden on a colleague, fostering teamwork. (Wow, we just demonstrated the first four ingredients in just one act!)

Luck

I was sitting at my desk in my spacious office in Philadelphia when the phone rang. I shouldn't have been there to receive the call; I was scheduled to conduct a training class all week. I know if the person on the other end of the phone left a message, I more than likely would have never returned it. I wouldn't have been interested. Since I was at my desk when the phone rang, I picked it up. The gentleman on the other end of the call introduced himself and said he wanted to speak to me about a job opportunity. He was a "head hunter" and somehow he set his sights on my head. Although I wasn't really happy with my current situation, I wasn't actively looking to make a move. But here I was sitting in my office with not much to do and no one around. I was bored, so I talked and listened.

He was looking for someone to head the training department of a small community bank located about a half-hour drive from my house. The bank had 6 branches, about 125 employees, and an asset size of $700 million. Best of all, I would be responsible for creating all of the training materials for the classes I was facilitating. I would have the authority and autonomy to do my own classes. I was intrigued and figured I had nothing to lose. I put a résumé together and sent it over to him. I made copies of recent projects I had accomplished including a massive redesign of a two-week teller training program which I had recently helped complete. I brought these materials to my interview to support my qualifications for the job. The longer the interview process went, the more I was interested in working for them as well as they were for having me. At the time it was the best interview I ever went on, and it all came to fruition because I was lucky enough to have my training class canceled and was sitting at my desk.

The moral of this story is; sometimes luck does play a supporting role in your advancement within your company. But as lucky as I was for receiving the call, I still had to seal the deal. If I bombed the interview, I know I wouldn't have gotten the job. My future, new bosses were impressed with the materials I gave them. Would it have cost me the job if I didn't bring them? If I didn't do a good job on the teller redesign, I would not have had anything worthwhile to show them in the first place. So while luck helped give me an opportunity, determination and hard work still got me the job.

3

PROMOTIONS ARE NOT SERVED AT THE DELI COUNTER

Let me begin by making a bold statement: I like food shopping. It's true. To start with, I like eating. Food shopping lets you decide and have complete control over which foods you're going to eat. Who wants to come home from a long day at work or school, open up the fridge only to find it's stocked with food you don't want to eat. While food shopping can sometimes be a hassle, it definitely is a lot easier on us than it was for our ancestors hundreds of years ago. Back then, you needed to hunt and gather. I don't mean hunt for sales and gather items in the cart.

Meats and poultry did not originally grow shrink-wrapped in Styrofoam. In this day and age, it is much easier.

Last Tuesday, I walked into my local supermarket to do some grocery shopping. While I was there, I went up to the deli counter to place an order. You know the drill. I saw the big red gadget with a slip of paper hanging out, and gave a tug on it. Out came a light blue ticket with a big red number 81 right on it. There, I had it, my number. I looked at the huge LCD screen on the back wall and it read 75. Right away, I knew where I stood. I was number 81, and the fine people behind the counter were already graciously helping number 75. My turn was coming!

It's great when you know your turn is coming. There is a sense of anticipation as the number gets closer. Seventy-six... seventy-seven. I search up and down the glass case, choosing what I want. A pound of domestic ham, low salt. A pound of smoked turkey breast...mmmmm. A pound of American cheese. Maybe some rolls, perhaps some fresh pickles... macaroni salad! I can sense my order, I can taste my sandwich. Seventy-eight... seventy-nine... eighty!

The woman with number eighty appears to be pushing eighty herself. She's an elderly woman with white hair and a blue jacket. She's unsure of what she wants. She changes her mind. Hey, that's her right; she's in charge. I know, because she's the one holding the light blue ticket; the ticket with the number which matches the one on the big LCD screen on the wall. Yep, she held complete control because it was her turn, and she was entitled. Now I'm getting excited. Why wouldn't I be: I was next.

Purchasing meats, salads, and such at the deli counter is simple. Everyone has a place in line; there is a natural order. The customer gets to choose what he or she wants, and gets their order delivered to them all with a smile from the employee across the counter.

Getting what you want at work is slightly more complicated than getting your way at the deli. Unfortunately, employees too often act like and believe the workplace should operate just like the deli. Employees frequently talk about "the list." Allegedly, sometime after you're hired, your name goes on "the list" for promotion. When an opportunity for promotion comes up, the manager breaks out "the list" and chooses the name at the top. Everyone else automatically moves up a spot. When your name gets to the top, you get the next available promotion. As a matter of fact, you are *entitled* to that promotion because... it's your turn.

Promotions are not served at the deli counter. In the corporate world, promotions are earned based on hard work, production, reliability, and personal growth. While experience is always a consideration for promotion, experience alone won't get you the job. Consider a baseball manager who manages in the minors for five years. When hired for the job, he was led to believe he is being groomed as a successor for the job at the big league club. During the five years his teams are terrible. They have a losing record each year, and his players are not as prepared for the major leagues as many scouts think they should be.

During the offseason, the manager from the parent club retires. The opening in the big leagues is finally here! Our minor league manager applies for the job. Would you promote him? He was on, and possibly at one time on top of, "the list." He has experience managing a baseball team. Unfortunately for him, his experience is managing losing teams full of underdeveloped players. Not the type of experience his bosses are looking for.

At the deli counter, the customers always stay in the same order in which they pulled their number. The deli workers will always serve number 87 right after they serve number 86, and before 88. Customers wait patiently in line with the knowledge and security their space in line will be unchanged. In the corporate world, employees have to fight to keep their space in line. You need to constantly prove you belong, and both your effort and production can either move you up or push you back further in line. Here is a concept I frequently teach employees in leadership training:

Very few stay the same. Either you are improving or you are getting worse.

Now I have had more than a few participants disagree with that last statement. People have argued they have stayed the same because they give the same effort, produce the same results, and achieve the same goals. Now I am not underestimating the production of these individuals. These are all commendable accomplishments. My concept isn't about how you compare to preordained goals and hard data. My concept is about how you compare to other people. If you are producing at the same levels, your progress is stagnant. If others increase their production to levels which meet or exceed yours then they are getting better, and by comparison you are getting worse. Don't believe me? Think about running a one-mile race. You get off to a great start and lead halfway through. You maintain the same speed the rest of the way, and still have a lead with 50 yards to go. Everyone else suddenly kicks their effort up a notch or two, and they blow by you in the last ten yards. At one time you were in first place, you maintained the same effort which got you in first, but you ended up in last place. So did you stay the same or end up worse?

There are many ways to improve at work. In this book I'm presenting you many principles to make you a better employee and more promotable. Let me give you three quick tips to look at right now.

1) **Read**. Remember the RIF program at school; Reading is Fundamental? It really is. Reading something every day allows you to discover new things and expand your knowledge. Reading exercises your mind and keeps it sharp; it's like doing pushups for your brain. Unfortunately, too many people are neglecting to take their brain for a

little book workout. According to a 2007 Associated Press-Ipsos poll published in the Washington Post (Aug 21, 2007), 27% of people polled hadn't read a book the entire year! The average person who did read a book had read four.[9] People need to read more – congratulations you are doing that right now!

I recently trained a class in which a 21-year old college student claimed he hadn't read a book since freshman year of *high school*. How is that even possible? I know the biggest excuse people make for not reading is they don't have the time. But you really do. Break a book down into chapters. It should take about 10-15 minutes to read an average book chapter. If you read a chapter a night, you'll have most books read in about two weeks. Don't have 15 minutes a day? You sure do. How much time do you spend on the internet looking at nothing in particular? How much time flipping through the channels on the TV without really watching a program? You'll find we waste plenty of time each day when we could be taking our brain for a workout.

What to read? You can read books, magazines, newspapers, it doesn't matter. It doesn't even have to be work related. Personally, I prefer biographies or books based on actual events to fiction. However, the truth is you can read books on any topic to get the benefit. In one of my classes I asked participants to write down the name of the last book they read with a brief one paragraph synopsis. I was able to show them how almost any book can be related back to a principle you can use in the business world. From the *Harry Potter* series, you can learn how to discover your secret skill and develop it to its fullest potential. This is a great lead into our second step.

2) **Discover your secret skill**. OK, get over the fact you are not really a boy wizard. So look for another secret skill. Seriously, everybody has one. What is the one thing you do best? In later chapters we'll discuss developing other skills you need to be more promotable. For right now, discover the thing you do best, and determine how you can maximize that in your current job. Are you extremely organized, able to do math quickly in your head, good with computer programs? The workplace is littered with many employees who excel at one specific thing while being mediocre at everything else.

I once knew a manager (let's call him Mr. A) who was very good at his job, but was inept at anything computer oriented. Mr. A was a member of our company's ALCO (asset/liability committee). In banking, ALCO controls the money; among other responsibilities they determine the weekly CD and loan rates. Mr. A was responsible for compiling a detailed report on our CD balances, terms, upcoming maturities, and peer rates. While Mr. A was good at deciphering data, he didn't know the first thing about how to create a spreadsheet in Microsoft Excel. So Mr. A did what any good manager would do, and delegated the responsibilities to one of his subordinates (let's call him Steve). Steve was great at extracting data from programs to create spreadsheets, filtering what was needed, and creating the necessary formulas to make the numbers fit. Steve loved computers. He got the job done quickly, and never had an issue whenever Mr. A asked for last minute changes (which happened frequently).

Yeah, Steve was great with Excel, but not with much else. Filing was not his passion, and the order of his files was not a representation of any alphabet I was involved with. He didn't enjoy calling customers on the phone, so his call list remained untouched on his desk from month to month. Steve frequently escaped the boredom of his job by taking frequent smoke breaks, which often irritated his co-workers. Regardless of his shortcomings in other areas, Steve was highly respected by Mr. A because he was able to do something the boss couldn't. His secret talent was discovered. Soon Steve's job changed. Any project which required extensive Excel work was given to him. Projects including Power Point and Access were quickly added too. Filing and customer calls were eliminated from his responsibilities. Steve went from a dead-end job he hated to one he enjoyed. His job description changed. He made more money – considerable more money.

3) **Find a mentor**. A long, long, time ago in a galaxy far, far, away lived a young farm boy named Luke Skywalker. Luke lived on the farm with his aunt and uncle; his mom had died during childbirth, and his dad suffered from what would now be referred to as the most intense case of personality disorder ever discovered. Anyway, Luke grew tired of his days on the farm, and dreamed of becoming a Jedi Knight. He knew this career path wouldn't be easy, so he set his sights on finding a mentor. Luke found a mentor in Obi-Won, and the rest was cinematic history!

Having a mentor, especially in the early stages of your business career, can be invaluable. A mentor can offer you perspective and experience, someone to bounce ideas off and vent, a little, and someone who can guide you through the office politics and let you in on company secrets. When looking for a mentor, obviously you want to find someone who has experience in the field in which you work, or are aspiring to work. Someone who is just as new as you is your friend, not your mentor. If possible, find someone with a background similar to yours. I progressed through my banking career with no college schooling whatsoever. For me, finding a mentor who also started as a teller straight out of high school gave me someone I could relate to more than a college graduate who started at a higher position. While you do want to find a mentor with similar qualities, his/her strengths should also be able to balance out your weaknesses.

Watch your mentor in action. Ask him why he did something or what thought processes he used in making a decision. Keep in mind a good mentor has developed respect within his field, so how he handles a situation may be different from how you should handle it. I had a younger employee who used me as a mentor while he was working his way up the ladder in a branch. Oftentimes when faced with a problem, he would ask how I would handle the situation. I would be quick to clarify if he wanted to know how I would handle it or how I thought he should handle it. You see, they were two different situations. Based on my position and level of respect in the organization, I was able to say or do something which would come out sounding confident from me, but likely arrogant coming from him.

One last thing about mentoring, and it's the most important. If you are serious about having a mentor, then you need to be serious about being someone worth mentoring. Take the person's advice seriously, and act as if you want to advance within the company. Good mentors are busy people, and they won't have the time to spend on someone who isn't truly interested in taking their advice and acting accordingly. When I first started officiating high school wrestling I saw a well-respected colleague of mine, Bill Stecklein Sr. in the stands. Bill was well-respected because not only was he one of the finest high school and college referees in the area, he was also a well known international referee. Bill has had the honor of officiating in four different Olympic Games, including being bestowed the tremendous honor of receiving the "Golden Whistle" award for outstanding officiating in the games. I asked Bill for advice and feedback that day I saw him in the stands and he told me one thing which has always stuck with me. He told me while he doesn't give his feedback often, he will when asked and is always completely honest with the officials. While he doesn't mean to be rude, he does mean to be thorough. He told me it does not benefit the official, coaches, or wrestlers for telling the official he had done a good job when there are obvious areas of improvement. I appreciated not only the feedback and advice Bill gave to me that night, but also for the perspective which allows me to provide detailed and honest advice to anyone who asks it of me in the future.

4

ALL I EVER NEEDED TO KNOW I LEARNED FROM BATMAN

In my humble opinion, the two most successful superheroes of all time are Batman and Superman. As a kid growing up in the 1970s, I spent my fair share of time watching reruns of classic superhero shows *The Adventures of Superman* and *Batman*. Many children grew up aspiring to be Superman; strong, indestructible, with the ability to fly, and see through most anything.

Now, who wouldn't want to be able to do all of that? However, Superman was not real. To start with, he was a comic book character. But even inside the world of comic books, Superman was not even human. He came from another planet. He was not Clark Kent who had a night job as Superman, he was Superman who had a day job as Clark Kent.

Batman however, was different; he was a real person (at least in the comic book world). Unlike Superman, Batman possessed no real superpowers. He is a mere mortal, just like you and me. Superman used his superpowers to fight for "truth, justice, and the American way." Batman had a cause and belief which drove him to develop skills to be productive. In a sense, Batman can be a role model for success in the workforce. Lessons learned from Batman can provide us with five basic rules to live by for becoming a successful employee.

Before we continue, if it appears as if you've read some of these rules before, you have – right here in previous chapters of this book. Issues such as hard work, opportunities, and teamwork have been previously discussed. But, they are important issues so they are worth repeating here in this chapter. Plus, if you didn't really buy into what I was talking about in previous chapters, maybe the Batman analogy will work better for you. Either way, here they are:

Batman Rule #1
It starts with hard work

As stated previously, Batman possesses no real superpowers. Instead, he relies on intellect, deductive reasoning, and technology to succeed. These are all important traits to possess, and are traits which are developed and honed over time. Let's discuss how you can put these traits to work at your job.

Intellect - It can't be bought, or taken like a pill. While some people are born with a higher capacity to learn than others, intelligence isn't a birthright. Intellect comes with experience, doing, or learning. In the workplace, employees are promoted because they excel at different areas within their department. Many start at an entry-level position with little prior knowledge of the job and work their way up through the ranks. Along the way they learn various important duties and responsibilities within their department. They attend training classes, read through procedure manuals, and ask questions.

Obviously, based on my profession, I am a huge supporter of attending training classes. Attend every training class you can, both internal and external – especially if it is free for you to attend. In my company, we offer classes on topics such as mortgages and other loans, IRAs, budgeting, credit scores, and more. I always try to impress upon new hires, many of them right out of high school, we are training you to provide service to our members; but along the way you are also learning valuable information you can use yourself. Working at a food store you learn how many different types of yogurt there are in the world. Working at a bank or credit union you learn how to invest for your future. Many employees who attend IRA training went back to their branch and opened up their very first IRA for themselves.

Deductive Reasoning – You do not need to be a detective to demonstrate deductive reasoning. In fact, most of your bosses will be happy if you demonstrate plain old reasoning or common sense. You learned at a young age if the stove is hot and you place your hand on top of it you will get burned. Common sense reasoning is to not place your hand on the top of a hot stove. Your employer expects you to take the same approach to common sense reasoning at work. If you think there is a problem, either fix it or let somebody know. If the copy machine suddenly stops making photocopies, there is a problem. If it's out of paper, then fill it up. If there is a jam, then fix it if you can. If you don't know how or are afraid you will make it worse, then let somebody know who is capable of fixing it. Do not just walk away and leave the problem to someone else. Eventually, your manager will discover you were the last one to touch the copy machine, and think if you are not capable to handle that, then you may not be capable of handling anything else.

Technology - One of the biggest advantages younger people have coming into the workforce is how much they tend to embrace technology. When I started in banking, employees reconciled checks with an adding machine, wrote memos with a typewriter, tracked working hours on a piece of paper, used a rolodex to organize contacts, and searched for the nearest payphone to make a call on their way to work! When I attended training classes, facilitators were on the cutting edge of technology if they made their own overhead slides. (For those who have no idea what an overhead slide was, let me take a moment to explain. The overhead slide was the ancient ancestor to a Power Point presentation. Words or graphics were printed on a clear plastic sheet which was illuminated on a wall by an overhead projector, which was a cross between a giant expensive light bulb and a magnifying glass. Instead of using custom animations to show the next line of text on the board, the trainer covered what they didn't want students to see by another piece of paper. It was very, *very*, cutting edge at the time).

Who knows how outdated the technology we use today will be within the next fifteen years. If you ever saw the Batman series from the 1960s, you'll remember Batman's computer system took up an entire wall in his Batcave. Today, that computer system would pale in comparison to the speed and content you can get from your iPhone. By keeping up with technology, you will always be a valuable asset to your company.

Batman Rule #2
You can't survive with only one tool

Batman is equipped with various tools to assist him to handle difficult situations. One of the most famous features of Batman is his utility belt. At one time or another, the bat-belt contained every tool and apparatus known to man (as well as a few which weren't). Batman knows not every perilous situation can be solved with a bat-a-rang or a bat-gripper. Batman needs to maintain a constant supply of tools in his belt to help him succeed at his job.

Good employees know there will be numerous challenges and obstacles which they need to overcome to be successful. All challenges are not the same and cannot be solved with the same response. Life is not a math problem; "x" does not always equal 5. Employees need to possess a wide assortment of tools to tackle the challenges and problems which come their way.

We have talked in previous chapters about taking advantage of opportunities to learn and develop new skills. Let's take a moment to look at some of the fundamental skills your employer expects you to possess:

- Basic skills such as being able to read, write, count, and perform simple arithmetic.

- Communication and listening skills.

- Personal skills such as working with others, serving customers, demonstrating integrity, being responsible, and respecting diversity.

- Thinking skills to be able to learn, problem solve, and make decisions.

- Technical skills – understanding computers and programs, how to troubleshoot when issues occur.

- Time management skills to arrive and complete deadlines on time, and work efficiently with limited supervision.

Your boss is expecting you to possess and use these tools in addition to others. Some tools can be trained such as dealing with difficult customers or using specific computer software. Others are expected of you when you get the job, such as basic math. Be honest when promoting your tools; claiming you posses something you obviously don't will eventually be discovered, and your supervisor may not appreciate your dishonesty. In most companies, providing false information on a résumé or job application can be cause for immediate termination.

I once interviewed for a job my junior year of high school at a large video store chain. It was a great job; watch videos all day and night for free, talk with customers, make some popcorn, and get paid all the while. It was a job I almost didn't get. You see while in high school I took two years of Spanish, passing each year with a solid 'D' average. On my application for the job under "Other Skills" I wrote down I could speak Spanish. Boy was I in for a shock when I got interviewed by the assistant manager, a nice Hispanic woman who spoke fluent Spanish! That became the first and last time I ever embellished my resume or job application.

Batman Leadership Rule #3
You need the help of your friends to win the fights

As impressive as Batman is, he still relies on the help of others. Batman could never handle all of his day-to-day responsibilities without the time management support of his loyal butler Alfred. He would be totally unarmed without those innovative tools we previously mentioned which were invented by Lucius Fox. Batman would surely not be able to beat up all of the bad guys without delegating some fighting to his trusty sidekick Robin.

Teamwork is another topic we've addressed in an earlier chapter. While we have mentioned the importance of why you should work together, here we will delve into understanding different types of people.

Well respected in the training and business world is the Merrill-Reid personality types method. According to Merrill-Reid, individuals can be categorized into four types of personalities: Driver, Expressive, Amiable, and Analytical.[12]

The **Driver** is a fast-paced, task-oriented employee who is motivated by success. These employees like doing things their own way; they are decisive and make strong leaders. This co-worker hates laziness and irreverence, so you better work hard and show respect around him or her. To work well with a driver, you would be best to support his/her goals. Do not get in the way or cause a distraction. When you see the guy in the office who is running back and forth from his computer to the printer, delegates effortlessly to his subordinates, takes charge in meetings, and celebrates the big victory – you have found the driver.

The **Expressive** is also fast-paced but is more of a people-oriented employee. This person is magnetic, enthusiastic, and friendly. He/she does not like routine indecision; if this employee were reading this line I would be chastised for typing he/she instead of making a commitment to choose one gender over the next. To work well with an expressive, you would be best to recognize the great idea he just had. It doesn't matter if you like it, doesn't even matter if it will get implemented or not, it just matters that it was great – and it came from him! The guy who comes up to you on your first day and says hello, the one who you can hear

100 yards down the hall, who wants to go out to lunch everyday – he's the expressive.

The **Amiable** employee is also people-oriented but works at a much slower pace. Much like a puppy dog trapped behind the window of a pet store, this person just wants to be liked, get attention, be accepted, and lick your face. (OK, maybe I stretched the puppy analogy with the last one there). The amiable is patient, reliable, steady, and modest. To get along with her, you must respect her feelings, check your ego at the door, and stay away from any conflict. When you see the employee who passes around the card for everyone to sign on your birthday, and brings in doughnuts just because it's Friday – you've found the amiable.

The **Analytical** employee is task-oriented and slow-paced. This person is motivated by substance, dependable, meticulous, and careful. She loves to ask questions and needs to see data to support your answers. To get along with her, you must be prepared to have exhaustive research to back up your comments. If not, allow her to look articulate and knowledgeable. If you truly want to win over an analytical just ask "how does that work" to any comment she makes, and be prepared for a ten minute detailed response. To locate an analytical in your office, head straight for the accounting or auditing department, they all live there.

Another important area of working with others is the ability to network successfully. *Networking* is interacting with other individuals in a business environment for mutual assistance or support. Networking can be used to seek advice or input, or share ideas. Networking can also be used to help in decision-making processes, which may include the decision to hire a new employee. As a word to the wise, you should always try to leave a job on the best possible terms. I've seen many instances where a recruiter for an organization has called a former colleague to ask about a specific employee, and the information received played a vital role in the decision to hire. When developing your personal network, look to include current or former co-workers, teachers, family, or friends.

Batman Leadership Rule #4
You have to stay fresh and embrace change

To stay successful over time, Batman has had to
consistently grow and change. Batman first appeared in
DC Comics in May 1939, and had his own comic the
following year. In 1966, the Batman character became
goofier with the debut of a prime time television series
starring Adam West. During the 1970s and early '80s the
popularity diminished, only to be resurrected by the 1989
movie starring Michael Keaton. After four major motion
pictures, and three different lead actors, the movies were
scrapped. In 2005, the series was repackaged with a
darker, more serious Batman.[13] Through all of its changes,
the 2008 *Dark Knight* became the highest grossing
Batman movie of all time.

Just as Batman can become stale and stagnate, so too
can your work performance. Employees who perform
rudimentary tasks may become bored quickly. Boredom in
the workplace can result in carelessness which can lead to
mistakes, increased absenteeism, gossip mongering, and
more. None of those situations will make you popular with
your bosses.

Embrace change and maintain a positive environment of change for your co-workers. Many employees are resistant to change: they follow the policy of "if it ain't broke, why fix it?" But companies usually change policy, procedure, computer systems, etc. to increase performance, profits, or control losses.

Working in the training department of a large commercial bank, I conducted conversion training on three separate occasions. "Conversion Training" is a nice way of referring to the training which occurs when one bank takes over another. The first two times I conducted this training was because my bank had just bought out another bank, and I was training their employees. In the last case, my bank was the one being acquired, and I had to train our existing employees. Few employees are happy when their company gets acquired by another. I was training branch employees, and 95 percent of the people I trained kept their jobs. While they had to learn a new computer system and new procedures, their basic job functions remained the same, and the people they worked with remained the same. The only change to their office was a new sign over the front door. Yet some employees remained upset, even outraged. More than one employee told me they hated change so much they were going to look for another job! Think about that for just a second. They hated change so much they were going to....*change* jobs. Incredible. Change is inevitable. You can either accept it and work with it or fight it. But it you fight it, that's a fight you're sure to lose.

Batman Leadership Rule #5
Be punctual

Whenever Commissioner Gordon displayed the "Bat Signal" over the skies of Gotham, he knew Batman would soon arrive on the scene. Batman understood the importance of being punctual; people were depending on him. Never once did Batman arrive late to a crime scene with the excuse he was caught behind a school bus!

Your employer needs you, and they need you on time. This includes reporting to work, returning from breaks, and completing assignments. Not only do your bosses need you to be punctual, so do your co-workers. Anyone who has ever worked shift work knows your shift can't end until the person working the next shift arrives. If you've already worked a long shift, the extra 20 minutes or so waiting for your replacement could seem like an eternity. In my work history, more people have been terminated due to attendance issues than any other single issue. If I can't depend on you to be on time, I may not be able to depend on you for other things either. If I can't depend on you, I don't want you working for me.

5

IT'S A (PAVLOV'S) DOG EAT DOG WORLD, BUT YOU DECIDE WHAT IS ON THE MENU

Dr. Ivan Petrovich Pavlov was a Russian psychologist during the turn of the 20th Century. Pavlov's main area of research throughout his career was on the digestive process, which led to his exploring the correlation between the nervous system and the autonomic functions of the body. Pavlov experimented with dogs, studying the relationship between salivation and digestion. By applying stimuli to the animals in a variety of ways, using sound, visual, and tactile stimulation, he was able to make the animals salivate whether they were in the presence of food or not. Dr Pavlov referred to this as conditioned reflex.[10] Scientists today refer to this also as behavioral conditioning.

The phrase "Pavlov's dog" is often used to describe someone who merely reacts to a situation as opposed to using critical thinking. Examples of the Pavlov's dog principle are found all the time in life, especially in the workplace. Imagine your supervisor asking you to come into his/her office and close the door behind you. If the only time employees are summoned this way is when they have done something wrong, your response would be feelings of nervousness, fear, and gloom.

The power of individuals over dogs is that they have the capability to decide how situations affect us. Our ability to think, comprehend, and evaluate allows us to understand the possible benefits and repercussions of our actions. Let's look at a quick scenario, and decide for yourself how you would react.

You are driving home from work alone. The road is busy, although there is enough room to maneuver and keep up with the speed limit. Another car races in front of you, cutting you off.

How would you react if this happened to you? Maybe you would yell at the driver and offer a few choice words. Perhaps you would display a hand gesture requiring only one finger to be pointing up. Even better, you would multitask and do both! These are common reactions to a hostile situation on the roadways; reactions which most of you would qualify as totally acceptable given the circumstances. However, would your reaction be the same if you weren't driving alone? What if your mom was in the front seat with you? Would it be the same if your five-year-old daughter was in the car? How about if you had just picked up three nuns hitchhiking at the side of the road right before you got cut off?

Most people would think about the other passengers in the car and curtail their reaction. This is proof our response was calculated and gauged, and not a spontaneous response. Between the event which transpired and the outcome, the driver chooses his or her response. The driver's actions were based on self-awareness and a quick determination of the repercussions of his/her actions.

There are repercussions for each and every action a person makes, or inaction a person chooses not to make.

While the word *repercussion* usually conjures negative connotations, they can be positive or negative. *Webster's Dictionary* defines a repercussion as an indirect or unforeseen effect of an event or action. With all due respect to Mr. Noah Webster, this definition is not completely accurate. Repercussions should not always be indirect or unforeseen. Everyone's action produces a result, and each individual should be acutely aware of any and all possibilities which may occur. Newton's Law of Motion tells us how every action has a complete and opposite reaction. This can be used in all areas of life, including the workplace. Let's look at another driving scenario to illustrate this point.

You are driving home from work and are in a hurry. It is around 5:30 and traffic is heavy in all directions. The light ahead turns red while you are still 30 yards away. You have a decision to stop at the light or drive straight ahead.

Of course you would stop. Failure to do so could result in an accident, causing severe injury and possibly death to you or to others. We understand the repercussions of our actions, and choose to act accordingly. Now let's change the details to the scenario above to 1:00 in the morning with nobody on the road. Would you stop for the light now? Would you look to see if a cop car was around and if a camera was affixed to the top of the light? Maybe we would blow the red light in this situation, changing our action from before. Realize we are still considering the repercussions of our actions, only this time the event has changed.

Remember high school algebra class where every problem required you to solve for a letter in an equation? If the teacher gave you the problem {X + 12 = 20} you would have to solve the problem to discover that 'X' equaled 8. Determining an appropriate response can also be like solving an algebra problem. In this case the equation would be listed below

$$E + R = O$$

Event + Response = Outcome

Event + response = outcome. When solving this equation, individuals need to solve for the value of their response. You have no control over the event. It is what it is. The *event* will always be either a past event or a situational reality. The *outcome* is the repercussion you are striving to have occur as a result of your action. The *response* is how you react to achieve your desired outcome based on the events presented.

In our first scenario, you were hurriedly driving home from work in heavy traffic when the traffic light ahead turns red. You can't control the light turning red. Your desired outcome is to get home as soon as possible without injuring yourself or others, or getting a traffic ticket. After considering the likelihood of causing an accident if you kept moving, you responded by stopping at the light. When we changed the event to eliminate traffic, we reduced the likelihood of an accident. This may have changed how you responded.

There are events which take place all the time in the workplace which require employees to respond. Employees are faced with many options all the time. This applies not only to work, but also in life in general. I want to present you with a concept which at first is hard to grasp – **everything in life is optional**. It's true. When I've trained this concept in classes the responses I get range from blank stares, to heads shaken in disagreement, to verbal challenges. "That's not true" is a favorite response... "I have to eat." Well, that's true to a point. Let's say you're home, it's dinner time, and you are served a meal you don't particularly care for. You have a choice – eat the dinner anyway, find something else to eat, or don't eat. You have options, and can choose to not eat. What would happen if you don't eat dinner that night? Depending what you ate earlier that day, you might feel hungry or maybe nothing at all. According to the Centers for Disease Control and Prevention (CDC), a 2007-08 study concluded 66% of all adults age 20 and over were overweight.[11] So perhaps skipping dinner isn't a bad thing for some people. So what if you decided the next morning you weren't going to eat the entire day? At some point you would probably start to feel the effects of not eating. You would develop a headache, feel sluggish, and start to lose focus. At some point you would have to start eating or else you would die of starvation. So when participants shout out "eating isn't optional, eventually if I don't eat I'm going to starve myself to death!" my reply is "it's all about understanding the repercussions of your actions."

OK, let's review for a moment: everything is optional, and event + response = outcome. When faced with a situation at work, you choose your actions and those actions have repercussions. Prior to making your decision you must consider what outcome your response will produce. Will it produce the desired outcome, and if not, is there a better response? If it won't produce the desired outcome, will it at least produce an outcome you can deal with? Too many times in work, employees respond to an event without thinking through the repercussions of their actions. They make decisions based on behavioral and emotional responses instead of thinking the situation through.

Let's talk about making decisions. People sometimes make bad decisions which result in negative outcomes, but sometimes negative outcomes are derived from good decisions. Let me explain. A decision should be judged good or bad only at the time it is made. There are too many intangibles which affect the outcome after the decision is made to fairly judge if it was good or bad at that time. Good or bad decisions should be judged based on all of the information the person had, or could have had access to, at the time the decision was made. For example, you get all dressed up and go outside without an umbrella – good decision or bad? Some people would answer "it depends on if it rains or not", but you can't say that. Raining is out of the individual's control. If the weather forecast was for rain, then it was a bad decision; regardless of whether the person saw the forecast or not. Remember, a decision is based on the information you had or *could have had*. You had the ability to see the forecast, you chose not to. If the forecast called for a sunny day and a shower popped out of nowhere, it wasn't a bad decision to not carry an umbrella, just a bad outcome to the decision.

Even if an employee makes the best judgment and responds in the most accurate way, the outcome can still produce an undesired result. This is the reason why you must work hard at solving the equation {E + R = O}. Just like in school, if you can do the homework and still get a poor grade, then you could really be in trouble if you skip doing homework altogether. Unfortunately employees sometime fail to do their homework in work. As discussed in other chapters, this is why we are left standing at the deli counter waiting for promotions, looking for our participation trophy for merely showing up each day, or spending most of the day complaining how work "just isn't fair." You have options to do or not do as you please. As the saying goes, "you reap what you sow."

All of the financial institutions I worked at have used some type of "mystery shop" to gauge the level of service employees provide to their customers. (In the fairness of full disclosure, I was once in charge of the mystery shop program of a small community bank). The shops are always done subjectively; the shopper had no pre-conceived notion of the employee they were shopping. In most cases, the employee was chosen completely at random. The mystery shop is intended to measure the level of customer service provided based on the standards of the institution. Employees are usually expected to get up and approach the customer, make eye contact, shake the customer's hand, provide their name, obtain and use the customer's name in discussions, answer any questions, etc. Over the years I can't possibly count how many employees failed to perform the basic skills of shaking a customer's hand and using their name, and then complain how unfair the mystery shop score was when they received it! When reviewing the mystery shops with employees, they would admit to not getting up, or shaking hands, or using the customer's name. When asked why, they would make up all types of excuses to justify their behavior. They chose not to follow the standard behaviors, and knew there could be repercussions for their actions, yet chose not to accept the repercussions once they came!

You can't have it both ways. You know what is expected of you and what happens when you choose to adhere, or not, to those expectations. Remember, everything is optional, but you are accountable for your actions. When I first took over the mystery shop program the shops were terrible. Employees didn't value the importance of the shop, and blamed everyone else for their low scores. "They make us shake customers' hands, and I don't feel comfortable doing that", I would hear. Well I don't know who *they* are, and even if I did, *they* don't make you do anything. That is proven by the result of the shop which states you don't shake hands. It's optional, and the repercussions of your inaction are a lower grade.

To illustrate this point I was invited to a meeting with all of the managers for all of the branches. The vice-president in charge of the branch network was present, as was my boss, the executive VP, and the bank's president and CEO. As we started our introductions I took a brand new package of dental floss out from my coat pocket, removed the packaging, and asked everyone to pass it around; ripping a foot or so of floss out when the container got to them. I had some really weird looks from members of my audience as this was being done. I asked the group how many of them go to the dentist on a regular basis and everyone's hand went up. I asked how many floss their teeth faithfully every single day. The managers looked at each other sheepishly before about one-third of the hands went up in the room. I used this opportunity to pick on a manager, Bill, who I knew well.

"Bill, are you aware the American Dental Association recommends flossing your teeth at least once a day, every day?" I asked

"Yes" was Bill's reply.

I continued, *"When you go to the dentist, does your hygienist remind you of the importance of flossing your teeth?"*

Bill responded *"Yes"* again.

"When you come home from the dentist, having your teeth feel all clean and nice, do you start flossing every day."

Bill acknowledged he does.

"How long does it last?", I asked curiously.

Bill chuckles, *"A couple weeks, then I kinda stop doing it."*

That was the response I was expecting, so I went in for the kill: *"Six months later, when the dentist's office calls to have you make your next appointment; what's the first thing you do when you hang up the phone?"*

"I go in the bathroom and floss my teeth!" was Bill's reply.

At this point the whole room laughs, but I made my point. It's no different when it comes to flossing your teeth, delivering quality member service, or performing any other actions and duties expected of you by your employer. You know what you are supposed to do, you know what is expected of you, yet it is up to you to decide what to do. Everything is optional. You just need to be ready to deal with the repercussions of your actions.

Promotions Are Not Served at the Deli Counter

6

YOU LIKE ME, YOU REALLY LIKE ME

Ed Rendell was the governor of the Commonwealth of Pennsylvania from 2003-2010. Before that, Gov. Rendell was the mayor of Philadelphia. Dubbed as "America's Mayor" by *Time Magazine*, Rendell oversaw the resurgence of the city after years of financial instability.

In the summer of 2008, almost halfway through his second term as governor, Rendell's approval rating was at 54% according to a poll conducted by Quinnipiac University.[14] Not too surprising for a governor who would answer to plain old "Ed" probably quicker than he would to "Mr. Governor."

The results of other questions in the same poll were surprising. When asked if they like the way he handles the state budget, only 40% of the voters responded yes. When asked about the controversial new plan to lease the Pennsylvania Turnpike to an outside firm, 60% **hated** the idea. Even worse, 63% hated the idea to toll Interstate 80, the longest east-west running interstate in all of Pennsylvania.[14]

How does a governor get such a high approval rating, when his three biggest initiatives are so widely unpopular? "It's his personality, his charm" says Clay Richards, assistant director at Quinnipiac University. "He can do no wrong even when he does wrong."

Never underestimate the likeability factor. People liked the governor. He was "one of them". On Sundays during the fall and early winter, Gov. Rendell would moonlight as a postgame analyst, dissecting the Philadelphia Eagles football games for the cable giant Comcast Sports Net. During the financial turnaround as mayor, Rendell would be present as the city's recreation department reopened pools which had been closed for years. There was Ed, taking off his shirt and doing a cannonball into the deep end.

Being well liked can help you in your career too. In all the financial institutions I have worked in over the years, the teller position was always considered an "entry-level position." Ask most branch managers, district managers, senior managers, and so on how they got their start in banking. A vast majority of them will say they started as a teller.

What are the requirements of a teller? To start, a teller needs to be able to handle money. At one time, the recruiters in human resources looked for someone with 'prior cash handling experience'. Many recruits got their cash handling experience working at grocery, department, or other retail stores. With the proliferation of credit and debit card use, cashiers handled more plastic than they did paper, so the cash handling experience wasn't as big a factor as it was before. Recruiters started putting a personal spin on their interviews. They started looking for more likeable candidates to become employees.

So what can you do to come across as likeable during your interview? I've worked with several human resource recruiters over the years and have acquired the following sure-fire tips.

> Arrive to your interview 15-20 minutes early. This shows you are a punctual employee (we've discussed the importance of punctuality in previous chapters). However arriving much more than this, say an hour early to the interview, may be an inconvenience to the employer. If you get lost on your way to the interview or are running late, call and explain the situation. The employer will understand and appreciate the notification. If you do arrive late, apologize for your lateness once you arrive.

> Dress appropriately. For most businesses this would include a shirt and tie for the men and suit or matching pant and blouse set for the women. Refrain from smoking or eating anything with garlic, onions, or strong spices prior to arriving. Also, don't try to cover it up with strong perfume or cologne. If you are chewing gum, lose it before you enter the building.

➤ Bring a notebook. This shows you are interested enough about the job to take notes. Also, prepare one or two questions for the employer. In an ideal situation you are interviewing the company as much as they are interviewing you.

➤ Offer a strong handshake and keep eye contact. Strong is not the same as a bone-crushing handshake, but it should not feel like the recruiter is shaking hands with overcooked pasta either. Maintain eye contact with the person interviewing you throughout the interview. You are not talking to your shoes, your notebook, or the clock on the wall during the interview – so you shouldn't be looking at those things.

➤ Show a personality. This doesn't mean to start the interview with a joke or magic trick, but lighten up. Consider the interview process like meeting your boyfriend or girlfriend's parents for the first time. Be willing to crack a smile and laugh at a joke.

➤ Use "we" as much as "I". When talking about accomplishments, don't forget to mention the rest of the team. Too much "I did this" during the interview can actually turn an employer off.

Recognizing others by saying "we did this" will still give you credit for the accomplishment as well as for being a team player.

Now that you have been hired and have the job, you still need to keep the likeability factor high to stay in everyone's good graces and be promotable. Here are four tips to keep your boss happy he hired you in the first place.

Maintain a positive demeanor.
I once heard famed speaker and author Zig Ziglar say "Some people brighten a room just by walking into it. Other people brighten a room just by walking out." I like that quote and use it often in my training classes. Maybe by now you've seen certain people at the office. I refer to them as "negaholics." They are the most miserable people you have ever known. These employees see the absolute worst in everything – doom and gloom. They are not happy unless they're unhappy. If one of these individuals won the lottery for $100 million, he or she would be complaining about having to pay the taxes.

For those of you having trouble spotting them, the negaholics may initially look harmless, walking through the door slugging their way towards the coffee machine in the break room. But then, like a cobra looking to strike, the negaholics will show the first sign of being dangerous in response to hearing those two threatening words: "good morning." Keep your guard up, as the negaholics can only get deadlier from there.

I had an opportunity to attend a training session conducted by a very engaging speaker, Larry Midgett. Larry refers to the negaholics as "E-Coli with shoes" because they are bound to spread their negativity to anyone who comes in contact with them. (Larry does extensive work with the United States government, and has NASA as one of his clients. Ever hear the phrase "You don't need to be a rocket scientist"? When Larry trains, sometimes you do!)

So if these people are so negative and can affect other people, one would wonder why they are still employed. Most likely it is because they have been in the workplace for a really long time, and when it comes to knowing procedures and processing work they are really good at what they do. Managers might regard these negaholics as indispensible despite their attitude. However, your manager probably won't feel the same way about you. A young, unproven employee who becomes a negaholic is just a pain in the butt to his or her manager. This person will be used as the sacrificial example to everyone else. So take my advice; be positive, or be unemployed.

Stay productive.

We were on a break from a class I was conducting when I heard a newer employee complaining about our policy which blocks social networking and game sites from being viewed on the internet. When I politely reminded her the company's internet access is meant to be used for business purposes she became a little belligerent. She asked if I knew how "boring" it was sitting in the office all day with nothing to do. After hearing her question I calmly asked my own; if her office was really so slow, why would we have needed to hire her in the first place? She just looked at me, obviously unhappy with my response. To this day I still don't think she got the point.

Nobody is entitled to a job. During 2009-2010, the unemployment rate hovered around the 10% mark.[15] Simply put, one out of every ten adults actively looking for employment couldn't find work. It's a safe bet if you aren't performing at the level you need to, then your employer can find someone else who will, possibly at a cheaper price. That's if your boss even fills the position at all. Companies throughout the country are expecting to do more with less. As an employee you need to stay productive; show your boss you are a value to the team, somebody worth keeping.

Embrace integrity.
Dictionary.com defines integrity as *adherence to moral and ethical principles; soundness of moral character; honesty.*[16] At my company, integrity is one of our three core values. Every quarter our CEO speaks to new employees during an all-day orientation session. When he speaks of integrity he lets employees know if they don't have it, they won't be in the organization for too long.

The easiest way to start demonstrating integrity in the workplace is to do what you say you are going to do. I've seen many instances where people make promises they can't keep. Even worse, people make promises they have no intention to keep in the first place. It's better to keep expectations low and exceed them than to constantly come short on what you said you were going to do. Keeping and delivering on promises not only show integrity, they also show dependability. Many of the supervisors I've worked with categorize their employees into two groups: those who are dependable, and those who are not. When it comes time to give someone a big assignment to complete, which type of employee would you think they would look to assign it? As we discussed earlier, that big assignment is an opportunity, and the undependable employees are going to miss out.

I provided you with the definition of integrity I found when looking it up on Dictionary.com. I tell people my definition is "doing what you are supposed to do when you could easily get away with doing something else." We all have responsibilities at work, and we should be aware of what we can or can't do. Most companies have detailed procedures which let you know what you can or can't do. Even if your company does not, I would bet your own determination of right and wrong will point you in the proper direction. I bet you've had a situation in work where you've said to yourself (or co-worker), "I wonder if I'll get in trouble if I do this?" Here is a helpful hint: if you are ever in a position where you are wondering if you should or shouldn't be doing something, you probably should not.

This is what I would refer to as making a wise decision. I've heard people say this: 'I know I shouldn't do this, but nobody will know." This is where real integrity comes in. If you know you shouldn't do it, but do it anyway because no one is watching, then you are lacking integrity. When you get caught and attempt to justify your actions, or try and point the blame at another direction other than your own, you are seriously lacking integrity.

Big banks love checking accounts, and as such most platform employees (those employee responsible for opening new accounts, taking loan applications, etc.) have checking account goals they must meet. Some employees would do anything to meet their goals; so much so they have done basically anything they had to do. One branch I knew operated as a kiosk inside of a supermarket. Employees would roam up and down the aisles approaching customers to open checking accounts. So far, this sounds like aggressive sales. However, these employees would have customers open $1 accounts, and would give the customer the $1 to open it up! These were bank customers in name only; no real relationship was formed, but the branch met their goals and employees received incentive payouts to boot!

The bottom line is, these employees were basically stealing money from the bank, and fudging numbers. There was no integrity in the way this branch met their goals. When they got caught (by the way, you ALWAYS get caught), they tried to justify their actions. It didn't work. The only thing that came out of the whole ordeal was a bunch of employees with short-lived banking careers.

Dress for the position you want.
One of my "other duties as assigned" was to go around to different departments and take employee photos which we used for our company's newsletter, annual meeting, or other events. Often I would get to someone's desk with a camera in hand only to be asked if I could come back the next day. It seems they were not properly prepared to have their picture taken for the entire organization to see. The problem may have been with their hair, makeup, or choice of clothing. Whatever it was, they were telling me they didn't look their best that day – and they knew it.

You may remember how you dressed for your first interview. You looked your best because you were trying to make a good first impression. You had a goal in mind; you wanted the job, and wanted the person sitting on the opposite side of the table to give it to you. At some point, while you are at the job, things change. Maybe you couldn't get to the dry cleaners this week, maybe you didn't have time to do your hair or makeup this morning, maybe you didn't feel like shaving. It really isn't a big deal, you figure. After all, you have the job and know everyone at work. Who are you trying to impress?

If you are trying to succeed at your job, then you should be trying to impress your manager each and every day. It doesn't make much of an impression wearing a nice clean suit to your interview for a promotion when every other day the same boss sees you looking like you just rolled out of bed. Look at the people in your office who are successful. (Remember when we discussed your mentor earlier?) Take your cues on dress and preparation from them. Multiple studies have shown when you look your best at work you usually feel your best and produce your best. Taking pride in your personal appearance will reflect in your work, and your manager will take notice.

Promotions Are Not Served at the Deli Counter

7

NOBODY WAS EVER RAISED BY WOLVES

I spent a little over a year as a trainer for a large commercial bank on the east coast. We had training centers which ran from as far south as Northfield, New Jersey to as far north as Bangor, Maine. "Ability to travel when necessary" was part of the job description, and I spent days training in various locations; sometimes for a day, sometimes for two weeks. During the first half of 2001, I had traveled and trained in 15 locations other than my own, from as far south as Northfield, NJ (20 minutes from Atlantic City), to as far north as Worchester, MA (near Boston).

While I always felt more comfortable and prepared in my home site, traveling gave me the opportunity to meet colleagues I didn't have opportunities to see too often. Plus the drive to some locations in New Jersey such as Pennsauken and Mt. Laurel only added an additional 20 minutes to my commute from the northeastern section of Philadelphia. Being assigned a few days in Northbrook, NJ gave me an excuse to visit Caesar's Palace and Trump Plaza. Spending a week in New York offered me the chance to walk out of the office and right into the sights and excitement of Times Square. I had an opportunity to spend my evenings watching *Phantom of the Opera*, *Rent*, and a young new magician trying to get his first break named Criss Angel.

Many times when I described the travel to friends and people I meet, they would tell me how lucky I was, and how they wished they had a job like mine. While the travel was fun, there were drawbacks which ultimately led to me leaving the organization. For starters, my dad was really sick at the time. I would often get voice messages on my cell phone from my mom informing me they were in the hospital. This left me to ponder a slew of thoughts lying alone in a hotel room in a foreign city. Even when dad was feeling well, there were other issues about the travel. While the company allowed overnight stay for some locations, other locations required me to commute. The company had a very strict "90/90 Rule" when it came to travel; if the commute was longer than 90 miles or took longer than 90 minutes, hotel accommodations would be provided. While the rule sounded fair, it wasn't practical. The "90/90" was determined by plugging the addresses of my home location and the site I was traveling to into *MapQuest* and accepting its calculations without exceptions. But according to *MapQuest*, my commute to Linden, NJ was 75 miles and should have taken me 82 minutes. Unfortunately, MapQuest must have never traveled northbound on the New Jersey Turnpike during rush-hour traffic! The commute was long and tedious, and class lasted for two weeks. The first week wasn't bad, but I was mentally drained come Wednesday of week two. For those of you who never stood in front of a class and facilitated for eight hours, it is a mentally demanding job.

The worst part of the travel had to be the fact I didn't have control of my own schedule. I was totally at the mercy of someone else. Around the middle of the month we received our schedule for the following month. One of my colleagues would joke whenever he received the email with the schedule he would automatically delete it, because he knew something better would come along. He was right. Revisions would get sent out, and trainers would be shuffled around. It would not be unusual to get three separate revisions in the same day! The main reason for the changes was some trainers didn't want to travel to certain locations or anywhere at all. By far the biggest excuse for being unavailable to travel was "I have a family."

I have been fortunate to have very good bosses throughout my career. My bosses have been people I learned from, who helped me develop as a professional, and who recognized a proper work/life balance. At the time I was traveling a lot, my boss Sylvia understood the need to travel, but also fought to keep us close to home as much as possible. (Unfortunately, while I reported to Sylvia the person who made the schedules did not.) Sylvia imparted me with one piece of wisdom I will always remember: "Everyone has family. Nobody was raised by wolves."

Sylvia was right on the money. Children being raised by wolves make for great movies and television, but it doesn't happen in real life. (Getting off topic a bit, somebody needs to bring back a good story about a child raised by wolves. I remember a show in the late 1970s called Lucan, in which a 10 year old boy was found being raised by wolves. When the series picks up, he's a young adult who needed to be trained to deal with human society. Whenever he got angry his eyes would glow a funky color and his animal instincts would take over; a cross between the Incredible Hulk and Teen Wolf. That was great stuff. A TV executive somewhere needs to bring that back).

As Sylvia's words sunk in, it marked the beginning of the end of the relationship with my employer. You see, I had to make a decision based on what was best for me. Between the travel, pay, and opportunity for advancement, it wasn't worth it. I needed to make a change, and I did.

While it is great to work for a boss and a company which values a proper work/life balance, ultimately your employer has expectations regarding your time at work. I understood my requirements were to travel. I didn't expect anyone was going to be able to lessen my travel. However, the time came when I felt I couldn't keep up the schedule anymore. I was no longer willing to make that sacrifice for my job. My needs had changed. I choose to look for another place to work.

In one of my leadership classes I train a principle to managers, supervisors, and future leaders. Although it is geared to leaders, it can be used by any employee to evaluate his/her current and perspective work situation. I didn't make it up, and perhaps you have heard about it someplace before. It's called the **NEWS** principle.

NEEDS

EXPECTATIONS

WANTS

SACRIFICES

Needs are the minimum, basic requirements the position provides you. When it comes to the job, your needs are non-negotiable. Needs can be based on finances (I need to make enough money to pay my bills), security (I need to work for a secure company who won't lay me off in a year), location (I need to be close to home, with limited travel), or hours (I need to be off on Sundays to attend church). It is important not to mistake your "needs" with your "wants." We will discuss your wants shortly. While you may want a job paying $60,000 a year, you can pay your current bills and be able to save while making only $40,000. As such, your needs would be a minimum salary of $40,000.

Expectations are your job requirements. Like needs, these are also non-negotiable; they are the needs of the company. In the corporate world, almost every company has a list of job requirements for each position. Where I work, prospective employees are given a listing of job requirements and a salary range during the interview process. They are also reviewed with employees every year during their annual performance appraisal, and discussed anytime they change. Employees must be aware of their requirements, be willing to perform the tasks, and expect the organization will hold them accountable for non- compliance. A few years ago our financial institution made a decision to implement Sunday hours, providing more convenience for our members to conduct their banking. Understandably, this decision was not popular with most of the men and women who worked in the branch network. Some employees decided to go elsewhere to work, which was completely their choice. Some employees stayed and complained about the new hours. They believed sometime soon management would change their mind and return to the practice of staying closed on Sundays. As of this writing, employees have been waiting for three years, and we haven't returned to the old schedule yet. Expectations are your job requirements; and if you are unable or unwilling to perform them it is time to look elsewhere for employment.

Wants are the things you aspire to achieve from your job. They are your goals, desires, or extra perks of the position. Wants can be based on finances, flexibility, position, or status. These are things which go above and beyond your needs; they are nice, but they can be sacrificed if push comes to shove. Having a computer which runs efficiently is a need, while having a top of the line computer with a 22" plasma screen is a want. You should list your wants in order of preference, and realize you may have to give up a want high on the list for three lower. While I was working for my previous employer, I had a spacious office with a sitting area to conduct meetings and a large sliding glass door you could close for privacy. When I left, I went to a job which offered me an open cubicle. Now I have to locate and reserve an available conference room to hold a meeting. However, I realized in the long run it didn't matter. While I wanted and enjoyed a big office, I was more than happy to trade it to be closer to home, have flexibility over my schedule, and the autonomy and authority to create and facilitate training programs which were important to me. Employees must understand the difference between wants and needs. To quote the old philosopher Mick Jagger, "You can't always get what you want, but if you try sometimes you just might find you get what you need".[17]

Sacrifices are the things which you are willing to give up to maintain your needs and acquire your wants. Ralph Waldo Emerson once said "For everything you have missed, you have gained something else; and for everything you gain, you lose something." Individuals need to decide what they are willing to lose in exchange for something gained. A person who goes back to school at night is sacrificing personal time; to spend with the family, partake in a hobby, or just unwind and relax. In his best-selling book *The 21 Irrefutable Rules of Leadership*, John Maxwell writes about the Law of Sacrifice: "there is no success without sacrifice". [18]

Employees need to evaluate their needs, wants, sacrifices, and employer expectations when making decisions affecting their career. If you are honestly unable to do something, that's ok. You know what your needs are, and what you have been asked doesn't meet your needs. If you are unwilling to do something, then that's ok too. It just means what you've been asked doesn't meet your wants; or maybe you are unwilling to make the sacrifices needed to accomplish a goal.

Oftentimes an individual's personal life, responsibilities, hobbies, and entertainment come in conflict with their work life. Those forty hours a week (plus travel) could be much better used doing something fun at home rather than being wasted at work. Perhaps your boss needs you to work the weekend but it's a nice summer day and you were thinking about taking a trip to the beach. Or, you have an assignment which needs to get completed today, but you have tickets to a game or concert and were hoping to leave early.

The biggest conflict between work and personal time involves issues of family. How many times has a parent been shorthanded at work only to receive a call from daycare informing her that her child is sick? This is a tough situation for anyone to handle. You really do have dual responsibilities to both work and family. Hopefully your boss can allow you to leave to care for your child, and your work will deal with being another person down. However, that's not always the case. Maybe a compromise is for your spouse, family member, or friend to pick up the child until you are finished work. There really is not a right answer on how to handle the situation. I've worked with a woman who decided when the call came from school her child was much more important than her job. She knew what her needs were, as well as what she was unable to sacrifice. As she was packing up she told me "If I get in trouble, I get in trouble. If I get fired, I'll find something else." She knew what was important to her, what her needs were, and acted on them. Consequentially, she received a written warning for her decision.

I have conducted classes on diversity from time to time. In the class we talk about different ways we are diverse from one another: age, race, gender, religion, marital status, family status, educational background, personal interests, and so on. I presented a situation to the class and asked them to make the decision individually. I then broke them into groups of three and had the group come to an agreement which they could all support. Here is the situation. Think for yourself what your decision would be.

> You supervise a group of four employees in your office, and it's Wednesday afternoon on a fairly quiet day. You have the staffing to send one person home early, and make an announcement letting the group know. Instantaneously, all four employees show up at your office door at the exact same time asking to leave. Each presents you with the following reasons why they'd like to leave:

- Sally wants to leave because it is her husband's birthday today. She wants to get a cake and surprise him with his favorite dinner.

116

- Rebecca has an important test at school tonight. She wants to get an extra hour or so to look over her notes.

- Matt has tickets to the baseball game. He wants to try and beat traffic before it gets too heavy.

- Eric just got a new puppy that has been locked in a crate all day. He wants to let her out and take her for a walk.

OK, you're the boss. Mr. or Mrs. Manager, who do you let leave early for the day? Hundreds of employees have attended one of my diversity classes over the years, and have had the same question presented to them. Over half of employees usually choose Rebecca. Their reasoning is she is going to school, and is bettering herself. Almost always someone in each class claims her reason for leaving early is "more important" than the others'.

This is where the real trouble begins. Rebecca's situation is more important to whom? Not to Sally, Matt, or Eric. Last I checked nobody's life is on the line. By ranking the importance of outside activities, the supervisor is going to have a real problem brewing in the office.

Remember, nobody was raised by wolves. Everyone you work with has some family – if not spouse and kids then parents, siblings, cousins, or friends. Everyone you work with has interests outside of the office. They all have reasons why they would prefer to be someplace else as opposed to being in the office. In most cases, your situation will not take precedence over someone else's. While a good manager should be sympathetic to your needs, the manager is still responsible for weighing the needs of the entire group over the needs of a single employee. If it appears as though one or two employees are being catered to, then there will be problems in the office. I can personally attest to this. If you are not the one being catered to then you will feel overlooked, undervalued, and begin to look for employment elsewhere. If you are one of the ones being catered to then it will be your co-workers becoming despondent and leaving. They may even start to resent you as they walk out the door. Employees who understand and appreciate each others' personal situations will go a long way to creating a good working environment. When you work in a good environment, everyone benefits.

7
WHAT WILL YOU DO WITH YOUR NEXT FOUR MINUTES?

I had completed the preceding six chapters in early 2010 as my wrestling season was nearing a close. I was on the mat for a sectional tournament semi-final match, where the winner advances to the finals and is guaranteed a spot in the following week's district tournament. The loser has to win two more consolation matches to advance. A wrestler from a team wearing green faced off against a wrestler from a team wearing blue. The match is near the end of the first period, scoreless, with not much happening. As both wrestlers near the out-of-bounds line, a flurry of action takes place resulting in the green wrestler on top of the blue wrestler as they both go out of bounds. This is one of those iffy calls where you as the referee are going to get grief from one side or the other regardless of your ruling. I ruled there was no control when they went out, no takedown awarded, and the wrestlers remain on their feet with the score tied.

Needless to say the coach from the green team is not happy with the call, and brings me to the scorers' table to discuss. I told him what I saw and felt, and said it was time to move on. Nothing he was going to say would make me change my call. Then I told him something I have never said to a coach before: "coach, it's still scoreless, your guy still has four minutes left to win the match."

I would honestly like to tell you how the wrestler from the green school battled back over the next two periods and won the match. But unfortunately that is not what ended up happening. No, the wrestler didn't do much of anything the rest of the match, and ending up losing 2-0. I could see his coach becoming more agitated as the match progressed. The takedown I never awarded would have been worth two points for him, so in his eyes I cost his kid the match. Of course, that is assuming everything else would have played itself out the same way and his wrestler would have found a way to win in overtime.

In this book I have attempted to provide you with tips and advice to help you succeed within the workplace. Principles mentioned here can help you in other aspects of life as well. We've talked about perceived fairness in the first chapter, and how in many instances you have the ability to make things happen for yourself, instead of relying solely on other people's actions and opinions. We've discussed how nobody gets rewarded for just showing up, and you cannot guarantee your place in line for promotions just by picking a number. I've told you everything you do at work is optional, but you need to understand and accept the ramifications for your actions – good or bad. We've also talked about how everyone has a life, personal interests, and responsibilities outside of work. Your situation is not more important than anyone else's.

If you have gotten this far in the book, then you have read and hopefully understood and appreciated all of the stories and words of advice I had to offer to you. That was actually the easy part. The difficult part is doing what comes next.

In my wrestling scenario earlier we all now know the wrestler from the green team had control over his destiny. His coach should have known it too. He was in a situation where he did not benefit from a decision (he didn't get awarded the takedown). He could have used the next four minutes to wrestle hard, execute his moves, and possibly win the match. Or, he could have chosen to dwell on the missed opportunity, do nothing more to help his cause, and use the situation as an excuse for losing.

He chose to make excuses.

What are you going to do with your next four minutes?

At the end of our workshops I talk about taking the next step. Training is the first step; you learn what needs to get done in order to reach your goal. When you take your first step you are pointing yourself in the right direction. You are starting to move ahead. But you haven't actually gone anywhere yet. To actually move ahead you need to take the second step – that's the key. All the training in the world won't help you succeed unless you are willing to use what you have learned to be more productive. That is the second step, putting the training to use. I ask participants to write down three things they will start doing, stop doing, and continue to do based on the training they just attended. On the following page is your opportunity to do the same based on what you have learned from reading this book.

After reading this book three things I will **start doing** are:

_____

_____

_____

After reading this book three things I will **stop doing** are:

_____

_____

_____

After reading this book three things I will **continue to do** are:

_____

_____

_____

In the first chapter of this book I mentioned taking the steps to become the obvious choice come promotion time, and referenced the book *Becoming the Obvious Choice* by Bryan Dodge and David Cottrell. If you have enjoyed reading this book I think you'll enjoy reading that one as well.

Now we are in the final chapter I want to reference another book I talk about in training, *The Dog Poop Initiative* by Kirk A Weisler. This is a children's book about a soccer coach who arrives at the field for an afternoon game. When he gets there he is warned by parents, other coaches, and officials about a large pile of dog poop in the middle of the field. Everyone is aware of the poop, has been careful not to step in it, yet has done nothing to remove it. The coach takes the initiative to find some cardboard from the trash and scoop up the poop and take it off the field.

The moral of the book is some people do a great job pointing out problems, while other people have the initiative to find a way to solve them. Pointing out the poop is easy. Scooping it up is not enjoyable, but it does produce results. And it can all be done in the next four minutes.

The moral of *The Dog Poop Initiative* sums up this book pretty well too. While confronting challenges at work, we have three choices:

- Do nothing and hope for the best, or
- Do nothing and complain when the outcome isn't to your liking, or
- Do something about it.

I hope this book has taught you the importance of doing something about it. Thank you for reading. I wish you success throughout your career.

Mike

REFERENCES

1) www.usconstitution.net/elec2000.html

2) www.presidentelect.org

3) Dodge, Bryan and Cottrell, David. *Becoming the Obvious Choice.* Cornerstone Leadership Inst, July 2001.

4) Smerconish, Michael. *Muzzled: From T-Ball to Terrorism – True Stories That Should Be Fiction.* Nelson Current, 2006.

5) www.brainyquote.com/quotes/quotes/t/thomasjeff104930.html

6) www.worldometers.info/weight-loss/

7) www.ushistory.org/franklin/quotable/singlehtml.htm

8) www.pro-football-reference.com

9) http://www.washingtonpost.com/wp-dyn/content/article/2007/08/21/AR2007082101045.html

10) http://nobelprize.org/educational_games/medicine/pavlov/readm ore.html

11) http://www.cdc.gov/obesity/data/index.html

12) http://www.bigideasnetwork.com/four_quad_personality_profile. htm

13) Daniels, Les. *Batman the Complete History. The Life and Times of the Dark Knight*. Chronicle Books, October 1999.

14) http://www.quinnipiac.edu/x1326.xml

15) http://data.bls.gov

16) http://dictionary.reference.com/browse/integrity

17) The Rolling Stones, "You Can't Always Get What You Want." By Mick Jagger and Keith Richards. *Let it Bleed*. 1969

18) Maxwell, John. *The 21 Irrefutable Laws of Leadership: Follow Them and People Will Follow You*. Thomas Nelson, September 2007 rev.

ABOUT THE AUTHOR

Michael Patterson has over twenty
years experience in the banking
industry; beginning his own career
straight out of high school as a
teller, and working in every branch
position.

Michael started training in 2000, and is currently
responsible for training and development of a $1.3 billion,
300 employee credit union in southeastern Pennsylvania.
He facilitates workshops on diverse topics such as
leadership, coaching, employee retention, and emotional
intelligence. Michael frequently visits schools to discuss
interviewing techniques and business ethics.

Michael lives in suburban Philadelphia with his wife Ann and their two dogs, Baleigh and Kimba. He is a registered Pennsylvania Interscholastic Athletic Association (PIAA) wrestling referee and former coach.

Michael is an active volunteer with Big Brothers/Big Sisters of Bucks County, PA. He is an avid sports fan and political junkie.

For more information please visit the
website

www.mikepat.com

Promotions Are Not Served at the Deli Counter